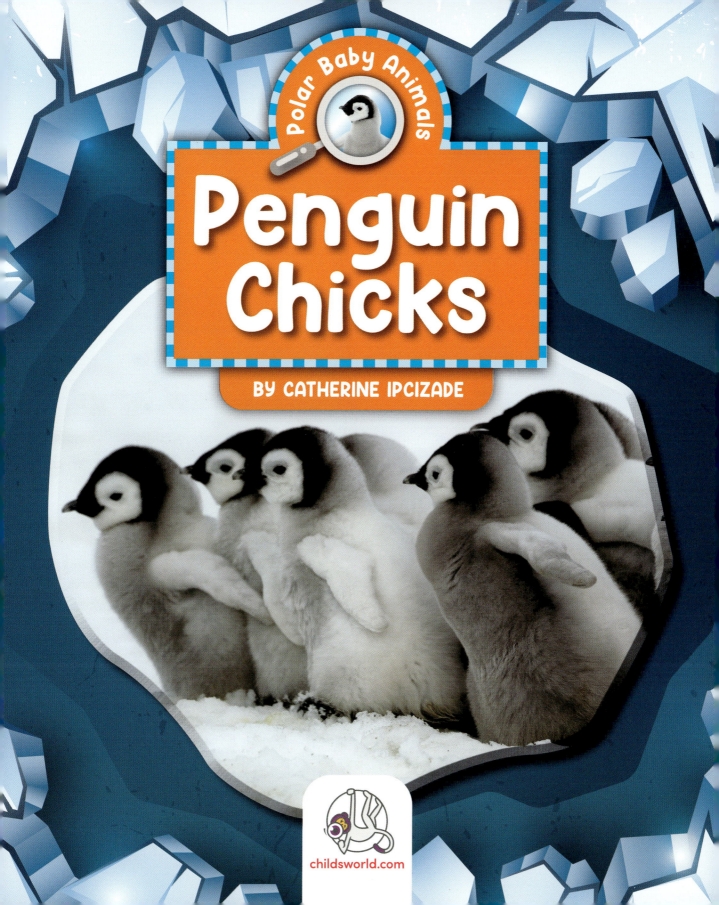

Published by The Child's World®
800-599-READ • www.childsworld.com

Copyright © 2026 by The Child's World®
All rights reserved. No part of this book may be reproduced or utilized in any form or by any means without written permission from the publisher.

Photography Credits
© Cover: ©Wolfgang Kaehler/LightRocket/Getty Images; ©Martin Ruegner/Stone/Getty Images; ©si_rubah_hitam/Shutterstock; page 2: ©Fuse/Corbis/Getty Images; page 3, 21–24: ©si_rubah_hitam/Shutterstock; page 5: ©Evgenii_Bobrovi/iStock/Getty Images; page 6: ©McDonald Wildlife Photography Inc./The Image Bank/Getty Images; page 9: ©Andrew Peacock/E+/Getty Images; pages 10–11: ©David Merton Photography/Moment/Getty Images; page 13: ©Svetlana Soloveva/iStock/Getty Images; pages 14–15: ©Natalia Shaw/500px/Getty Images; page 17: ©Snowdrop/iStock/Getty Images; page 18: ©Paul Souders/Stone/Getty Images; page 22: ©Chase D'animulls/Shutterstock

ISBN Information
9781503870772 (Reinforced Library Binding)
9781503871410 (Portable Document Format)
9781503872653 (Online Multi-user eBook)
9781503873896 (Electronic Publication)

LCCN
2024951061

Printed in the United States of America

About the Author

Catherine Ipcizade is a college professor and the author of more than 40 books for children. She loves photography, cooking, and spending time with her family in sunny California and the mountains of Utah. Her favorite word is "serendipity" because life is full of unexpected, fortunate surprises.

TABLE OF CONTENTS

CHAPTER 1
Hello, Penguin Chick! . . . 4

CHAPTER 2
Welcome to the Family . . . 7

CHAPTER 3
Feeding Time . . . 11

CHAPTER 4
Growing Up Penguin . . . 12

CHAPTER 5
Play and Explore . . . 15

CHAPTER 6
Staying Safe . . . 19

CHAPTER 7
Becoming a Penguin . . . 20

Wonder More . . . 21
Penguin Habitat . . . 22
Glossary . . . 23
Find Out More . . . 24
Index . . . 24

CHAPTER ONE

Hello, Penguin Chick!

A penguin chick uses its **flippers** to swim through freezing waters. **Icebergs** float all around it. This is Antarctica. It is the coldest place in the world, and it is where many penguins call home.

　　Penguins are birds, but they don't fly. They have flippers instead of wings. All penguins look similar. They have big heads, short necks, long bodies, and **webbed** feet. They are mostly black and white. There are 18 **species** of penguins. Each species has its own color pattern. Emperor, Adélie, gentoo, and chinstrap are a few penguin species. There is even a macaroni penguin.

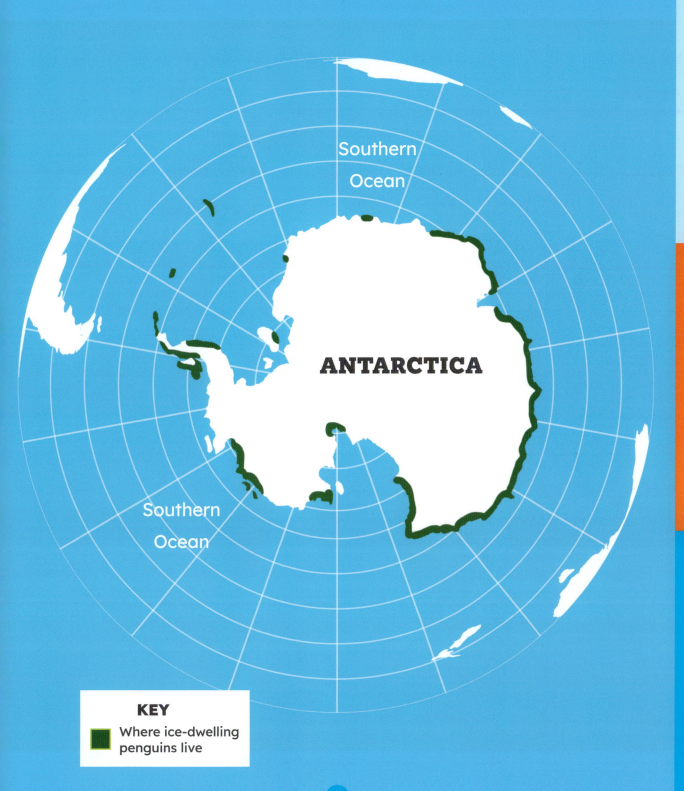

Penguins tuck their eggs under a flap of skin called a brood patch to keep them warm.

CHAPTER TWO
Welcome to the Family

When it is time to **mate**, male penguins create a nest. They make a call known as a trumpet. This sound attracts the female penguin, and she begins to trumpet also. A few days later, the female penguin lays one or two eggs. Both penguins take turns sitting on the eggs to keep them warm.

One to three months later, the eggs are ready to hatch. The chick pokes a small hole in the egg with its beak. Then, it works to break through the shell. This can take up to three days.

Penguin chicks are fragile when they are newly hatched. Their parents must keep them warm. Some penguin chicks grow **waterproof** feathers in around seven weeks. Others don't grow waterproof feathers until they are a year old. Until then, penguin chicks cannot survive on their own.

Once they have their waterproof feathers, penguin chicks are ready to **forage**. When penguin chicks can swim, their parents leave them to find food and survive on their own.

All About Feathers

Adult penguin feathers **insulate** them from the cold. But to keep them working properly, penguins must **preen** their feathers often. Penguins twist and turn their bodies in the water. They rub their bodies with their flippers. Penguins also preen by producing oil on their tails that they rub over their feathers.

Penguin chicks do not have waterproof feathers when they are young and must stay close to their parents for warmth.

Some penguin species must feed their chicks regurgitated food for about three months.

CHAPTER THREE

Feeding Time

Penguin chicks cannot feed themselves when they are newly hatched. The mother and father take turns feeding the chicks. The parents swallow food. Then, they **regurgitate** the food into the chick's beak.

Not all penguin species eat the same foods. But they are all carnivores. This means they eat meat. Penguins eat krill, squid, and fish. Chicks must learn to find this food in the water in order to survive to adulthood.

CHAPTER FOUR

Growing Up Penguin

Penguins are social animals. They live in **colonies**. Colonies can include many thousands of penguins. Penguins help one another survive. They swim together and even eat together. They may hunt together as well, but some penguins prefer to dive for food by themselves. Some penguins even huddle together in groups to keep warm.

Baby vs. Adult Size Comparison

The emperor penguin is the largest penguin species. It stands 3.5 feet (106.7 centimeters) tall. It can weigh up to 90 pounds (40.8 kilograms).

Emperor penguin chicks weigh 11 ounces (311.8 grams) when they hatch. They stand about 6 inches (15.2 cm) tall.

The markings and colors on penguin chicks are different from adult penguins. As chicks grow, their colors and markings change.

Calling Out to One Another
Penguins have similar markings. This may make it difficult for parents to quickly recognize their young. But parents do not need sight to recognize their penguin chicks. Instead, they rely on unique vocal calls to find one another. It's kind of like a secret song!

CHAPTER FIVE

Play and Explore

A penguin chick enters the water. It takes a deep breath, and then it dives! For a penguin chick, each day is an adventure. They explore every day. They wobble and fall. They quickly learn to walk and to swim.

Penguins are playful. They huddle together for warmth. Sometimes, the huddles look like dancing. The large colonies provide penguin chicks with many playmates.

Penguins are fast swimmers. Their long, oval-shaped bodies help adults to swim about four to seven miles (6.4 to 11.3 kilometers) per hour. It takes chicks time and a lot of practice to swim this fast. Since penguin parents do not stay with their chicks very long, young penguins practice swimming on their own.

Penguins' bodies are heavy. To swim, penguins must flap their flippers rapidly so that they do not sink. Penguins cannot breathe underwater. Special air sacs help them to stay underwater for long periods of time.

Emperor penguins can hold their breath for about 30 minutes at a time.

Penguins swim, dive, and hide to avoid predators such as leopard seals.

CHAPTER SIX

Staying Safe

Penguins have **binocular** eyes that can see clearly on land or in the water. This helps them find food or spot **predators**. They do not have many land predators. This is important since penguins cannot fly. But penguins must avoid predators in the water, such as seals and killer whales.

Their color pattern also helps them avoid predators. It is called countershading. Their feather pattern looks like a suit. This camouflage hides penguins as they hunt in the water for prey.

CHAPTER SEVEN

Becoming a Penguin

When they are between five and eight years old, penguins are ready to mate and create new penguin chicks. They find new colonies and create their own nests. Smaller penguin species may live six years. Other species live up to 30 years.

During their lifetime, penguins help the planet. As they move from the water to the land, their waste helps mosses and other plants grow. This supports the **ecosystem**. Without penguins, seals and other penguin predators might not have enough food. Penguins keep the **food chain** active and provide valuable resources in and out of our waters.

Wonder More

Wondering About New Information

Write down two facts that you learned about penguin chicks. What surprised you about those facts?

Wondering How It Matters

Penguins live in colonies. Why is this important? What would happen if penguins were solitary and could not huddle together for warmth?

Wondering Why

Why do you think it is important for penguins to live in places with few land predators? What might happen to the penguin population if they lived in areas with many land predators?

Ways to Keep Wondering

After reading this book, what questions do you have about penguin chicks? What can you do to learn more about them?

Penguin Habitat

You Will Need:

- shoebox
- construction paper
- cotton balls
- glue
- markers
- plastic toys (penguins, seals, etc.)

Steps to Take:

1. Lay the shoebox open on its side.
2. Glue cotton balls inside the shoebox to decorate it like Antarctica.
3. Using what you've learned researching penguins, use the paper and plastic toys to represent a penguin's habitat, including icebergs, snow, and water. Tip: Cut blue construction paper into squiggly strands to look like water and waves.

Glossary

binocular (by-NOK-yoo-lur) Binocular eyes face the same direction and can focus on an object at the same time.

colonies (KOL-uh-neez) Colonies are groups of animals or people that live together.

ecosystem (EE-ko-sis-tum) An ecosystem is a community of living things and their environment functioning as a unit.

flipper (FLIP-pur) A flipper is a broad, flat limb on fish and some birds that is used for swimming.

food chain (FOOD CHAYN) The food chain is the arrangement of organisms in a community in order of what eats and what gets eaten.

forage (FOR-uj) To forage is to look for food.

iceberg (IYSS-burg) An iceberg is a large floating mass of ice detached from a glacier.

insulate (IN-soo-layt) To insulate is to keep warm.

mate (MAYT) When animals mate they join together to produce offspring.

predator (PREH-duh-tur) A predator is an animal that lives by hunting other animals for food.

preen (PREEN) To preen is to groom, smooth, and shed feathers.

regurgitate (re-GUR-juh-tayt) When an animal regurgitates, it spits up chewed, undigested food in order to feed its young.

species (SPEE-sheez) A species is a group of living things that are able to reproduce.

waterproof (WAH-tur-proof) When something is waterproof, it prevents water from getting in.

webbed (WEBD) Animals with webbed feet have skin between each toe to help them swim faster.

Find Out More

In the Library

DeNapoli, Dyan, and Ray Shuell. *All About Penguins: Discover Life on Land and in the Sea.* Emeryville, CA: Rockridge Press, 2020.

Jones, Mark, Tui De Roy, and Julie Cornthwaite. *Penguins: The Ultimate Guide.* Princeton, NJ: Credo Reference, 2022.

Sill, Cathryn P., and John Sill. *About Habitats: Polar Regions.* Atlanta, GA: Peachtree, 2021.

Williams, Kathryn. *Hello, Penguin!* New York, NY: National Geographic, 2017.

On the Web

Visit our website for links about penguin chicks:

childsworld.com/links

Note to Parents, Caregivers, Teachers, and Librarians: We routinely verify our web links to make sure they are safe and active sites. So encourage your readers to check them out!

Index

calls, 7, 14
colors, 4, 14, 19

eggs, 6–7

feathers, 8–9, 19
flippers, 4, 9, 16
food, 8, 10–12, 19–20

iceberg, 4

swimming, 4, 8, 12, 15–16, 18